JOHN TYLER

JOHN TYLER

A PRESIDENT OF MANY FIRSTS

by

Jane C. Walker

The McDonald & Woodward Publishing Company

Blacksburg, Virginia

2001

The McDonald & Woodward Publishing Company
P. O. Box 10308, Blacksburg, Virginia 24062-0308

John Tyler : A President of Many Firsts

© 2001 by Jane C. Walker
All rights reserved
Printed in the United States of America by
Victor Graphics, Inc., Baltimore, Maryland

First printing January 2001

08 07 06 05 04 03 02 01   10 9 8 7 6 5 4 3 2 1

Library of Congress Cataloging-in-Publication Data

Walker, Jane C.
  John Tyler: a president of many firsts / by Jane C. Walker.
    p.cm.
  Includes bibliographical references and index.
  ISBN 0-939923-81-5 (alk. paper)
    1.   Tyler, John, 1790-1862. 2. Presidents—United States—Bi-
  ography. 3. United States—Politics and government—1841-1845.
  I. Title.

E397 .W35 2000
973.5'8'092—dc21
[B]
                                                          99-052917

Contents

Acknowledgments

For the past three years I have thoroughly enjoyed researching and writing this biography of John Tyler. My enjoyment not only comes from my love of history, but also from the warm reception I have received from the Tyler family and the staff at Sherwood Forest Plantation. Their time, support, and valuable information have added depth to this book. I am greatly obliged to John Tyler's grandson, Harrison Ruffin Tyler, and his wife, Payne Bouknight Tyler. For helping me to prepare the book and photographs of Sherwood Forest, I am grateful for the assistance of the managing director, Kay Montgomery Tyler, and her staff. I also thank Anne Tyler Netick of Charles City, Virginia, for permission to reproduce the portrait of John Tyler on the cover of this book and John Tyler Griffin of Devon, Pennsylvania, and Mrs. Tyler R. Stuart of Orinda, California, for permission to reproduce the color portraits of Letitia Christian Tyler and Julia Gardiner Tyler, respectively. William G. Clotworthy kindly permitted me to use his collection of official engravings of the presidents in several places throughout the text. Finally, I would like to thank my daughter, Robin Walker, for drawing the figures of John C. Calhoun, Henry Clay, and Daniel Webster.

Introduction

The catchy slogan "Tippecanoe and Tyler, Too" helped Tippecanoe's war hero, William Henry Harrison, win the United States presidential election in 1840. A month into office Harrison died whereupon " . . . Tyler, Too" — John Tyler — became the tenth president of the United States. Tyler was the first vice president in American history to succeed to the presidency upon the death of a president, and in so doing he established the precedent for presidential succession that is still in use today in the United States.

Coming into office as he did, Tyler's right to be president was challenged. Yet, despite the often severe criticism and other significant adversities he faced during his four years in office, Tyler maintained his claim to the office, held strong to his political beliefs, and persisted in attending to the responsibilities of the presidency. As a result, his administration accomplished several important objectives in domestic affairs and foreign relations, among the most important of which were the settlement of many festering disputes with Great Britain, the establishment of diplomatic relations with China, and the annexation of Texas.

The story of John Tyler is that of a nation wrestling with its own identity and attempting to answer profound moral, economic, and political questions as the country struggled to come of age. It is also the story of a man who stubbornly defended a vision of the American republic nurtured during his father's generation, even as America pursued a different dream. The America which existed at the time of Tyler's death in 1862 bore little resemblance to the country into which he was born in 1790. In essence, John Tyler's life is the story of

America's adolescence. By understanding the forces of change that were unfolding in Tyler's time and the ways in which he reacted to them, we can better recognize and appreciate the contributions to America made by this remarkable gentleman from Virginia.

Born into Politics

George Washington was still in his first term of office and the United States was largely agrarian when John Tyler was born on March 29, 1790, in Charles City County, Virginia. He was the sixth of eight children born to Judge John Tyler and Mary Armistead Tyler.

Tyler's Youth

Tyler's youth was spent on a 1200-acre estate — a plantation called Greenway because "its grass doth grow so green" — lying along the north side of the James River. There, under a large willow tree, Judge John Tyler often played his fiddle and told stories of the Revolutionary War to his children and the children of his slaves. Tyler loved music and he, too, began to "fiddle" at an early age. As a boy and as a young man, Tyler learned the values and social graces expected of a Virginia gentleman.

Young John Tyler's mother died when he was seven years old. Friends of Tyler believed him to be much like his mother: soft-spoken and gentle-mannered. After his wife's death, Judge Tyler never remarried, but he bestowed upon his children a great deal of love, guidance, and support.

Despite his gentlemanly nature, John Tyler could be quite headstrong in matters of right and wrong. When he was ten years old, he had a school teacher named William McMurdo. McMurdo was knowledgeable, but he was also very harsh and often used birch switches to whip his students unmercifully. One day, John and a few other boys got tired of McMurdo's whippings so the boys attacked him, threw him down to the floor, and tied his hands and feet. They then proceeded to leave the school building and lock the door behind them.

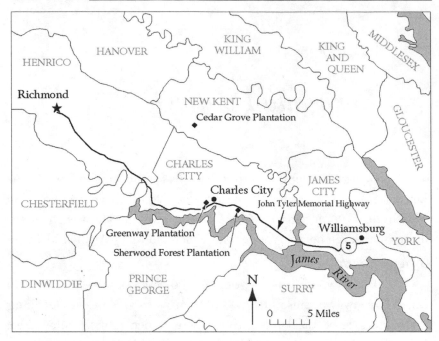

John Tyler's Virginia. Most of John Tyler's personal and public life was centered on that part of the commonwealth between Williamsburg in the east and Richmond in the west.

Some time later, a traveler found the angry, embarrassed, and still bound schoolmaster, and released him. McMurdo then stormed over to Judge Tyler and told him what had happened. Judge Tyler, who knew the schoolmaster well, shrugged his shoulders and said only, *"Sic semper tyrannnis,"* that is, "Thus always to tyrants."

Tyler's Political Inclinations

Judge Tyler was a father and a plantation owner, but he also was a politician who served as a state and federal judge and governor of Virginia. His close friend and college roommate was Thomas Jefferson. He and Jefferson enjoyed hearing discussions at the capitol in Williamsburg, Virginia, and it was here, as the new United States came into existence, where many of Judge Tyler's republican beliefs were formulated. This republican ideology, championed by Jefferson and others, held that the national government should be given only limited powers in order to prevent the development of tyranny which could result if the central government were too strong. On the other hand, according to this line of reason, the states should retain sovereignty over their internal affairs.

John Tyler followed in his father's footsteps and in 1807, at the age of seventeen, graduated from the College of William and Mary. Like his father, young John had an interest in law and politics so he studied law and was accepted to the bar. However, he would practice law only intermittently during his life.

At the age of twenty-one, Tyler got his first taste of politics when he became a member of the Virginia House of Delegates in 1811. Around this same time, while attending a party, Tyler met the beautiful Letitia Christian, the daughter of Robert Christian of Cedar Grove Plantation in New Kent County, Virginia.

Letitia was a quiet and reserved young woman whose delicate features added to her femininity. The two fell in love and courted according to the strict rules of conduct expected of a Virginia gentleman. It has been said that Tyler did not dare kiss Letitia's hand until three weeks before their wedding, which took place on March 29, 1813 — Tyler's twenty-third birthday. Marrying into the Christian family, whose prominence equaled that of the Tylers, also helped the young lawyer's social and political life.

John and Letitia's marriage was a happy one. They built a plantation home, called Woodbourne, in Charles City County, on land adjacent to Greenway, John's childhood home. Six years later, John purchased Greenway.

Although Letitia saw to the operation of Greenway with the help of overseers and very much enjoyed the work, this responsibility nonetheless was very demanding. She supervised most of the housekeeping, cooking, sewing, and nursing of both her family and those of the house servants and field hands. So great were her responsibilities that she chose to stay in Virginia when Tyler, elected to fill a seat in the United States House of Representatives in 1816, went to Washington.

Tyler in the House of Representatives

John Tyler served five years in the House of Representatives, from 1816 to 1821. Because the salary of a United States Representative was meager at that time, Tyler rented a room in a modest boardinghouse in Washington, DC, during sessions of Congress, which lasted roughly from November until March. Like many politicians in Washington, Tyler typically would not see his family from the time a session started until Congress adjourned and he could return home.

During Tyler's years as a representative, Washington was a swampy, malaria-infested city. Livestock roamed the unpaved streets. Both the Capitol Building and the Executive Mansion were in the process of being rebuilt — in August, 1814, during the War of 1812 both buildings had been set ablaze by the British Army. To cover the charred bricks of the president's home, that building was painted white and eventually acquired the nickname "The White House."

Being from a prominent Virginia family had its advantages for the freshman congressman. Within weeks of his arrival in Washington, Tyler was dining with President James Madison and his wife Dolley, whose attempts at preparing French cuisine Tyler detested. While the social life in Washington was grand, the work of a congressman frustrated Tyler. The Jeffersonian model of limited government and states' rights was gradually being eroded by the Nationalists, who sought to create a stronger and more active federal government at the expense of state sovereignty.

The Nationalists

The years after the War of 1812 brought about significant changes in America. The population of the country increased, and transportation improved with the building of roads, canals, and railroads. In New England, farms gave way to factories as a manufacturing economy emerged. Domestic and foreign demand for the agricultural products of the South increased. And, growing numbers of Americans and immigrants began to move west — across the Appalachian Mountains and into the Mississippi Valley. America was becoming a nation, rather than a union of individual states, and this change was reflected in the political debate that characterized the period from 1814 to 1825.

The American System

Throughout his early life, Tyler adhered to his father's view of the limited role of the national government. He sought to protect the sovereignty of the individual states, a position made clear in his speeches and with his votes as a congressman. In contrast, however, some politicians with other views— called Nationalists — were coming to believe that America needed a more robust national government.

One prominent Nationalist was Henry Clay of Kentucky, the Speaker of the House. The influential Clay proposed a tariff on certain imports that would protect the emerging industries of the Northeast, he wanted federally financed internal improvements and a national bank, and he supported western expansion. He called his view on national issues the American System, and its goals were to increase domestic trade, connect the expanding country through turnpikes and

Henry Clay

canals, and stabilize the currency. Clay believed that his plan would bring about increased commerce, and it would make the United States less dependent economically upon Europe.

Tyler did not support the American System. He believed that the nation, which was created at the signing of the Constitution, was designed to have a weak central government and that the United States was to be a confederation of individual states. Tyler also recognized that the tariffs imposed by Clay's American System favored manufacturers in the Northeast while they restricted the ability of southern planters to sell their goods overseas.

The National Banks

The first National Bank was created in 1791 by President Washington's Secretary of State, Alexander Hamilton. In eighteenth-century America, banking was largely unregulated, and states and individual banks had been free to issue their own currency. Hamilton had hoped that having a national bank would regulate money, which in turn would allow Americans to conduct business more easily. Hamilton's opponents, such as Thomas Jefferson, had argued that it was unconstitutional for the national government to operate a bank.

On April 10, 1816, Congress passed a law creating a second National Bank. By 1819, three years after its inception, the bank was in financial trouble, a circumstance which gave its opponents an opportunity to abolish it. Tyler — who, like Jefferson, felt that a national bank was unconstitutional — was appointed to a five-man congressional committee to investigate the bank's problems. As he laboriously read through folios, ledgers, and other financial records, Tyler learned the reasons for the bank's distress — mismanagement, violations of its charter, and corruption among the directors of the bank.

Tyler presented his analysis of the bank's difficulties, but he failed to persuade his colleagues in government that the bank had been mismanaged and should be dissolved. Two months later the Supreme Court upheld the constitutionality of the National Bank; the bank corrected its financial problems and resumed business. The failure of efforts to bring an end to the National Bank was a disappointment to Tyler.

Attempted Censure of Andrew Jackson

"Old Hickory," as Andrew Jackson was called, had been an army general serving on the southern frontier of the United States in 1818. In retaliation for depredations on American settlements by Indians from Florida, Jackson — following, and perhaps exceeding the intent of, unclear orders — invaded Spanish Florida, killed hundreds of Creek Indians, captured the town of Pensacola, and executed two British citizens who were accused of inciting the Indians. This action constituted an unauthorized invasion of a foreign possession; it created a national embarrassment and diplomatic problems with both Spain and Great Britain. The House of Representatives moved that Jackson be censured, a motion which Tyler strongly supported. "Old Hickory," however, was a popular hero, especially in the western territories, and the motion to censure him went down to defeat. Tyler, however, would never again trust Andrew Jackson and, over the ensuing years, his dealings with Jackson were generally disappointing.

The Missouri Compromise

The year 1820 brought mixed blessings to Tyler. Much to his relief, a restrictive tariff bill, opposed by the southern states, was defeated. The debate over Missouri's statehood, however, eclipsed all other matters before Congress and the nation, and became a markedly controversial issue for the national government at the time and for years thereafter.

The issue before Congress was whether to admit Missouri to the Union as a slave state. Politicians from the North did not want new slave states admitted, and in opposing Missouri's admission as a slave state, they attacked the morality of slavery itself and effectively politicized the institution at the national level. Tyler and other representatives from the South insisted that the national government had no right to regulate slavery. They recognized that there were problems with the practice but they believed that it would gradually disappear as it was doing in the northern states.

The controversy over Missouri's admission ultimately was ended by the Missouri Compromise of 1820, which was proposed by Henry Clay. Clay, a slave owner himself, suggested that Missouri be admitted as a slave state and that Maine be admitted as a free state. This would preserve the existing numerical balance between slave states and free states and their representation in the Senate. The compromise also divided the new western territories at the parallel of thirty-six degrees, thirty minutes —an east-west line essentially corresponding to the northern boundary of Arkansas. Slavery would not be permitted in territories north of this line. Territories south of the line could, if they wished, permit slave holding.

Pleased with himself, Clay believed that the slavery issue finally had been settled. Tyler, however, thought differently. He saw the compromise to be unconstitutional and was convinced that the dispute would persist.

John Tyler became discouraged over the frustrations he experienced while serving in Congress. His efforts to preserve state sovereignty in the face of the Nationalists' initiatives had largely failed. Exhausted, Tyler came down with a digestive disorder, which he might have contracted by eating spoiled fish in his boarding house. So serious was his illness that he was plagued with gastrointestinal problems for the remainder of his life.

Home to Virginia

In order to recuperate from his illness, Tyler resigned from Congress on January 15, 1821, and returned to Woodbourne, Letitia, and his ever-growing family, which now included three children. His daughter Mary had been born in 1815. She had been followed by Robert in 1816 and John, Jr., in 1819. Later, in 1821, another daughter, Letitia, was born. Eventually, Tyler would father fifteen children — more than any other American president.

John Tyler recovered from his illness, managed his plantation, and, by 1823, returned to politics — once again serving in the Virginia State Legislature. Like his father in the previous century, John was elected by the Legislature to become the state's governor. In 1825, he and Letitia moved into the Governor's Mansion in Richmond, only to discover that the governor's salary was insufficient to cover the social demands of the office. Letitia went to great lengths to keep the social functions modest, but the state government simply did not provide enough money for them to meet the social expectations of the office without contributing money of their own.

Tyler suggested that they hold a banquet for the members of the Legislature. They would be served Virginia ham, cornbread, and cheap whiskey — fare consumed by the common people of the state. He hoped that such a meal would call to the guests' attention the need to increase the governor's salary. The banquet was given and the guests ate their meal, but the salary increase never materialized. Tyler's strategy had failed to elicit the additional necessary funds from the state government.

Consistent with his belief in state sovereignty, Governor Tyler proposed many initiatives to improve education, transportation, and commerce in Virginia. He suggested that Virginia provide public schools for all classes of people, and he encouraged the Legislature to provide funds for the building of canals and roads. Tyler had seen how DeWitt Clinton, the governor of New York, had been successful in getting the Erie Canal built. Thus, in Tyler's mind, a state could financially manage internal improvements without the aid of the federal government.

Tyler Returns to Washington

Prior to the passage of the seventeenth amendment in 1913, United States Senators were chosen by their state legislatures. In 1826, the term of Virginia Senator John Randolph was about to expire and the state legislature was to vote on whether to return him to the Senate. One day before the scheduled vote, a group of anti-Randolph legislators nominated then-Governor Tyler for the seat. Tyler won the election by a slim margin, resigned his office as governor, and returned to Washington — this time as Senator Tyler.

In 1828, John Quincy Adams once again ran against Andrew

John Quincy Adams

Jackson for the presidency. President Adams, whose political leanings clearly were Nationalist, had proposed many federally funded programs for internal improvements. Because of Jackson's opposition to Adams's Nationalist views and policies, Tyler — who similarly opposed Adams — reluctantly supported Jackson. The campaign of 1828, marred by name-calling and mud-slinging, ultimately was won by Jackson. Tyler knew that the opportunistic, reckless Jackson would cause a stir in Washington, but on that account "Old Hickory's" arrival exceeded even Tyler's expectations.

Crowds of rough, drunken, plain folk filled Washington to celebrate Jackson's inauguration. After the inauguration, an open reception at the White House was turned into a spectacle of crashing glass, damaging furniture, and whiskey-drinking pandemonium. To protect what remained of the White House and its contents, the servants were forced to move the food and drink onto the lawn.

After the raucous inauguration, Jackson set about attending to the work of the presidency. Among his policies was support for states' rights, and from 1829 until 1831, Tyler supported and praised the Jackson administration. Despite Jackson's flaws, his administration was, to Tyler, a welcome change over the nationalistic programs of former President Adams.

However, Tyler's enthusiasm for Jackson eventually would abate. His distrust of the president resurfaced as a result of Jackson's implementation of tariffs and his handling of disputes over the constitutionality of the National Bank.

The Doctrine of Nullification, or "interposition," that became a heated political issue during the late 1820s and early 1830s was

Andrew Jackson

championed by John C. Calhoun of South Carolina. The Doctrine of Nullification, when fully developed, asserted that states could interpose their sovereignty between that of the national government and the citizens of their own states. In so doing, state legislatures could vote to nullify acts of Congress within the borders of their states. At the heart of the nullification issue was opposition among southerners to the national tariff acts passed by Congress in 1828 and 1832. These acts imposed protective tariffs on certain goods, including some textiles, which protected Northern manufacturers while angering many southerners. South Carolina — with Charleston, the South's most important cotton port and intellectual center on the Atlantic coast — was not pleased with either tariff. On November 24, 1832, South Carolina attempted to nullify the tariff acts and threatened to secede from the United States if the federal government attempted to force the collection of these tariffs. Angry and threatening exchanges followed between President Jackson and the governor of South Carolina. Calhoun, who was Jackson's vice president, resigned his office in protest and was appointed to an opportunistically vacated seat in the Senate in order to better serve the interests of his home state in Congress.

John C. Calhoun

As Tyler had feared might happen, "Old Hickory's" military inclinations had re-emerged. Angry and frustrated, Jackson sent a naval force to Charleston Harbor, and army troops were prepared to take military action against South Carolina to enforce collection of the tariffs. As tensions mounted, Tyler, in a private conversation with the well known master of compromise Henry Clay, asked Clay to visit with Calhoun and try to negotiate an acceptable resolution to the growing problem. Clay and Calhoun were indeed able to forge a workable compromise, and their agreement was adopted by Congress as the Compromise of 1833. The crisis ended without bloodshed but the

regional economic differences that were behind it, along with the slavery issue, remained as festering cracks in the national unity. The resolution of the crisis pleased Tyler, but his suspicions of Jackson persisted.

Like Tyler, President Jackson believed that the National Bank
was unconstitutional despite the Supreme Court's earlier decision that
the bank *was* constitutional. Jackson's position was controversial and
not entirely logical, since only a national bank could issue paper currency that could circulate throughout the nation and maintain a relatively stable value, but his views did have a fair amount of support.
Jackson, fearing both the political and economic power of the National
Bank, decided to force its closure by removing federal funds deposited
with the bank. If the federal deposits were removed, Jackson reasoned,
the bank would quickly become insolvent and fail or, at least, would
be greatly weakened. After a protracted search for a Secretary of the
Treasury who would authorize and legally defend the removal of the
federal funds, Jackson found Roger B. Taney to be the man who would
try to carry out his will. While Congress was in recess in 1833, Jackson ordered that the federal funds be withdrawn from the National
Bank and transferred to the twenty-three state banks. He justified this
action by claiming that he was saving the people from wicked bankers.
In truth, the bank had grown stronger since its re-establishment in
1816, the transfer of funds from the National Bank had been more to
satisfy the popular perception that banks were evil institutions than
to improve the financial stability of the nation, and the action contributed to the panic of 1837.

The unauthorized withdrawal of money from the National
Bank angered Tyler and many other politicians. Although he opposed
the National Bank, Tyler believed that the president had no right to
arbitrarily and unilaterally bring down an institution created by Congress and vindicated by the Supreme Court. He was convinced that
the doctrine of separation of powers had been violated. Yet, even though
the Senate passed resolutions condemning the president's actions, Jackson had succeeded in closing the bank.

Because of this incident, Jackson's enemies dubbed him "King Andrew I." In retaliation for the administration's actions against the bank, Tyler and others who opposed the president asked for censure of Jackson and Taney, the imposition of limits to presidential veto power, and constraints on the president's authority to make appointments.

The Virginia Legislature favored Jackson's states' rights policies and supported his withdrawal of funds from the National Bank. The Legislature, which had elected Tyler to the Senate, instructed Tyler to vote against the censuring of the president. At this time, many state legislatures believed that they had the authority to instruct their Sena-

King Andrew the First, an 1832 lithograph critical of the authoritarian president.

tors how to vote on specific issues — a matter upon which the Constitution was actually silent.

Tyler believed that the Virginia Legislature did have the authority to issue "instructions," and that he was obliged to follow them. However, he could not in good conscience support Jackson's policies. For this reason, Tyler resigned from the Senate and from the Democratic party, choosing principles over politics.

Jackson was not censured and the public funds remained in the state banks. These banks, in turn, printed paper money that flooded the nation as prices rose rapidly.

Vice President Martin Van Buren succeeded Jackson as president but, unfortunately, he inherited the Panic of 1837 — a financial collapse which was largely a result of Jackson's banking policies. On May 10, 1837, New York City closed its banks and two days later, the banks of Philadelphia closed. The panic spread throughout the country and caused business failures, loss of markets for farmers, and rising unemployment. The country was in a depression and President Van Buren, whose banking and other policies were closely linked to those of Jackson, received much of the blame for the country's financial straits.

The Election of 1840

In 1834, a new political party called the Whigs had formed. The party adopted its name after the British Whig party which stood for limiting the power of the monarch. The American Whigs were

primarily men who opposed the banking policies of Andrew Jackson, who they referred to as the United States' monarch. With the economic depression that began in 1837 and the resulting financial distress of the nation and political embarrassment of the Van Buren administration, the Whigs had a real opportunity to win the presidential election of 1840.

In keeping with Jackson's popular

Martin Van Buren

frontier theme, the Whigs chose another veteran with experience in the western territories, an elderly politician named William Henry Harrison. While governor of Indiana Territory, Harrison had led a military force against Shawnee Indians encamped at the mouth of Tippecanoe Creek. On November 7, 1811, Harrison's camp was at-

President Martin Van Buren being put out of the White House as William Henry Harrison takes up occupancy, a lithograph from the 1840 presidential campaign.

tacked by the Indians, but they were subsequently repulsed and their nearby village was occupied. Although militarily insignificant, the Battle of Tippecanoe became well known and Harrison became its hero.

Choosing a candidate for vice president proved more difficult for the Whigs. They were certain that they could not win the election without strong support in the South. In order to gain votes from the Southern Democrats who disliked President Van Buren, they chose John Tyler — by now one of those "turncoat Democrats" who politically favored states' sovereignty along with the Southern Democrats, but disapproved of their party's current shady deals as exemplified during the Jackson and Van Buren administrations. Tyler had always put principles before politics, and thus he accepted the vice presidential nomination. After all, the vice president at this time was a relatively unimportant office; even if elected, Tyler could serve his four-year term residing with his family at his Virginia home. The Whigs were pleased with Tyler's acceptance, believing that they had found winning candidates who would implement their nationalistic agenda. They would be gravely disappointed.

Uncle Sam herds Jackson, Van Buren, and Mother Bank into a hard cider barrel held in place by presidential candidate Harrison — an 1840 woodcut.

Tyler, Too

The presidential campaign of 1840 was unlike any that the United States had seen before. Lacking any defining issues, the Whig party copied Andrew Jackson's tactics and turned the election into a frontier hoopla. Parades, posters, banners, log cabin floats, songs, and hard cider excited and enthused the crowds. Many who attended the rallies knew little or nothing about the issues, the Whig party, or its candidates.

The Election of William Henry Harrison

William Henry Harrison was promoted by the Whigs and campaigned as a candidate of the people. Pictures abounded showing him in populist and western scenes, often seated by a log cabin with a barrel of cider nearby. Equally appealing to the masses was what would become one of the most enduring campaign slogans in American presidential history — the alliterative and easily remembered "Tippecanoe and Tyler, too!" Vying for public attention, Whig enthusiasts engaged in such spectacles as rolling giant ten-foot-wide balls from town to town, and state to state, shouting "Tippecanoe and Tyler, too!"

John Tyler, the Virginia gentleman, was unsuited to a populist campaign of this type. He was uncomfortable wearing a coonskin cap and felt awkward when speaking to masses of common people. Moreover, the "folksy" nature of the campaign reminded him of Andrew Jackson — so, as a result, he spent minimal time campaigning.

The Democratic party under Jackson and Van Buren had controlled the White House for twelve years. However, the depression of the late 1830s and the Whig's frontier populism and national republi-

HARRISON
AND
TYLER.

MAJ. GEN. WM H. HARRISON.

N. E. CONVENTION,
SEPTEMBER 10, 1840.

Images from a campaign ribbon used in the 1840 presidential contest.

canism helped to sweep Harrison and Tyler into the White House in 1840 in what was largely an issueless campaign. William Henry Harrison, who received 234 electoral votes to Martin Van Buren's 60, was now president, and John Tyler, the new vice president, removed himself to Williamsburg.

The aging Harrison had worked hard during the 1840 election campaign, and his demanding schedule had weakened him considerably. Shortly after his inauguration he contracted pneumonia and, after serving only one month in office, died on Sunday, April 4, 1841. No United States president had ever died while in office. The Constitution provided that, upon such an event, the vice president was to assume the duties of the president, but it did not state whether he actually would become president. Some believed that the vice president would function only as an "acting president" until an election could be held to select a new president.

Understanding the gravity of the situation, Harrison's Secretary of State Daniel Webster sent his son, Fletcher, and an officer of the Senate to Williamsburg, Virginia, to inform Tyler of the president's untimely death. On the morning of April 5, 1841, the two messengers awakened Tyler and informed the vice president of President Harrison's demise. Stunned, Tyler decided to leave immediately for Washington and instructed his son Robert and his daughter-in-law Priscilla to join him a week later. Tyler's wife, Letitia, now partially paralyzed by a stroke, was to remain at home until she was strong enough to make the journey. The youngest children would come with their mother.

Tyler quickly left with the messengers and traveled to Washington, arriving in the city early in the morning of Tuesday, April 6. Based upon his interpretation of the Constitution, Tyler claimed all of the rights and privileges of the presidency, and was sworn in as the tenth president of the United States on April 6 at the Brown Hotel in Washington.

Tyler Assumes the Presidency

Not everyone accepted Tyler's interpretation of the Constitution on the matter or manner of his ascending to the presidency. Among his fiercest opponents were those of his own party, the Whigs, who had placed Tyler on the ticket to attract Southern voters to the Whig camp — not to make him president. The thought of John Tyler, the staunch supporter of state sovereignty, as president of the United States angered many in his party. Inspired by Henry Clay — who himself had twice sought the nomination of the Whig party for president and who continued to harbor aspirations for the office — the Whigs began to refer to Tyler sarcastically as "His Accidency" in hopes of demeaning him.

The period from 1820 to 1840 has been called the "Golden Age of the Senate" in recognition of the disproportionate influence on national politics wielded by three powerful senators known as the "Great Triumvirate" — Henry Clay of Kentucky, Daniel Webster of Massachusetts, and John C. Calhoun of South Carolina. All three were well established politicians who, by 1840, held highly evolved and strongly developed views on issues of national importance. Two of these men — Clay and Calhoun — were in Harrison's cabinet when he died and were inherited in that capacity by Tyler when he assumed the presidency.

Clay made no secret of his opposition to Tyler and the two were at odds from the outset of Tyler's administration. Despite the fact that Clay had a reputation as a heavy drinker, a womanizer, and a gambler — vices that may have prevented him from ever being elected president — he was a brilliant and charismatic Nationalist whose golden voice seemingly could persuade even his harshest enemies. He was

Tyler's unprecedented ascent to the presidency and his differences with Henry Clay and the Whig party generated much criticism and ridicule for the tenth president during his term of office.

well aware of his political savvy and would use it, combined with other devices such as ridicule, to achieve his goals. As a result, Tyler's first year in office was a stormy one. Twice Clay charmed enough votes from Congress to pass bills that would establish another National Bank, and twice Tyler vetoed those bills. Clay then tried to pass legislation that would create protective tariffs, and again every effort ended with Tyler's veto. Politicians and others stopped calling him "His Accidency" and began to refer to him as the "Veto President." The press, which had supported the Whigs, vehemently attacked the president and his unpopularity grew. The influenza epidemic that spread across America at this time even became known as "Tyler's Grippe."

In an extreme case of focused public anger, a mob once stormed across the White House lawn, hurled stones through the windows, shouted insults, threatened assassination, and burned an effigy of the president. Still crippled by a stroke, Letitia trembled in her bed as Tyler and the servants stood by with their guns and guarded the White House until the mob dispersed.

On September 11, 1841, Tyler became "a president without a party." Under Clay's influence, and largely as a result of differences over the banking legislation, every member of the cabinet, which had been appointed by Harrison, resigned with the exception of the Secretary of State, Daniel Webster. For Tyler, the resignations were an embarrassment but they were also a blessing since the cabinet had been more loyal to Henry Clay than to him, their president. With their resignations, Tyler could fill the cabinet with trusted men who shared his political ideals, and for a president to be able to work successfully with Congress, a capable, effective, and loyal cabinet was essential. Daniel Webster, in particular, proved to be invaluable to Tyler — in his conflicts with Henry Clay as well as in important affairs of state.

Although Clay might have had a golden voice, Webster was an accomplished orator who could move politicians and others on the great issues of national unity and well being.

Remaining in Tyler's cabinet had been a noble and courageous act for Webster, but opposing Clay had put Webster in an obviously awkward position within the Whig party. Tyler admired and appreciated Webster's loyalty to his country and, although

Daniel Webster

they differed in their political views, they respected each others' talents and became good friends.

Letitia's Death

The year 1842 was a bittersweet one for John Tyler. Letitia never regained her strength following her stroke, and during her entire residence in Washington she left her bedroom only once — when her daughter Elizabeth was married in the White House. On September 10, 1842, Letitia died, and a funeral service was held for her at the White House on Monday, September 12. Cabinet members, senators and representatives, family members, and friends listened while the rector of Saint Johns Episcopal Church eulogized an honorable lady. Letitia was buried in her family's cemetery at Cedar Grove Plantation, her childhood home in New Kent County.

John Tyler, the reserved Virginia gentleman, was grief-stricken and the White House became a gloomy place. Social activities were kept to a minimum, and to assuage his loneliness, Tyler purchased a 1600 acre plantation in Virginia called Walnut Grove for $10,000 and shares of stock in the Kanawha Canal Company. Walnut Grove was located on the north bank of the James River, a little less than four miles east of Greenway. Tyler dove heavily into remodeling and expanding the plantation house, and in 1843 he renamed it Sherwood Forest. He chose the name because he felt that he, like Robin Hood, had achieved a sort of outlaw status.

Tyler the International Statesman

Though an outlaw in domestic politics and within the Whig party, Tyler proved to be very capable in dealing with representatives of other nations. His diplomatic, genteel manner and conversational ability appealed to foreigners and contributed to his several successes in international affairs. Indeed, some of Tyler's most important accomplishments as president came in the area of foreign affairs.

Daniel Webster had chosen to remain temporarily as Tyler's Secretary of State in order to finish negotiations with Great Britain which would define the boundary between British America and the United States and resolve several other matters that were under dis-

Greenway Plantation, birthplace of President John Tyler. Built in 1776 by Judge John Tyler, President Tyler purchased the property in 1821 and lived there with his first wife Letitia Christian Tyler until 1829. (Courtesy Sherwood Forest Plantation)

Letitia Christian Tyler (1790–1842) was the first wife of President Tyler. They were married in 1813, and she died in the White House in 1842. (Courtesy John Tyler Griffin and Sherwood Forest Plantation)

Julia Gardiner Tyler (1820–1889) was President Tyler's second wife. She served as first lady during the last eight months of Tyler's presidency. (Courtesy Mrs. Tyler R. Stuart and Sherwood Forest Plantation)

John Tyler in Washington. This portrait, painted by Hart in 1841, is owned by The Library of Virginia and hangs in the Virginia State Capitol. (Courtesy The Library of Virginia)

One of the many political campaign posters from the popular and colorful 1840s "Tippecanoe and Tyler, Too" presidential campaign. (Courtesy Sherwood Forest Plantation)

The dining room at Sherwood Forest Plantation features china used in the White House during President Tyler's administration and architectural details and wallpaper selected by Julia Gardiner Tyler. (Courtesy Sherwood Forest Plantation)

The explosion of the Peacemaker cannon aboard the navy's new frigate Princeton *on February 28, 1844, as depicted in a contemporary lithograph by N. Currier. (Courtesy US Navy Museum)*

pute or otherwise contentious. Tyler worked closely with Webster as he and Lord Ashburton of Great Britain sought solutions to the troublesome issues. During a difficult moment in the negotiations, Tyler requested an interview with Ashburton. The president's polished manners eased Ashburton's anxieties and allowed Webster, now discouraged and in ill health, to resume working with his British counterpart until the points of conflict were resolved.

The results of these negotiations were incorporated into the Webster-Ashburton Treaty of 1842. The most important issues resolved by this treaty were that the northern boundary of the United States was fixed from the Atlantic coast of Maine westward to Lake of the Woods, some two-hundred-fifty miles west of Lake Superior; that the United States would implement naval patrols off the west coast of Africa to assist the British Navy in curtailing the slave trade; and that procedures were established for the mutual extradition of suspects accused of committing crimes of violence and crimes against property. More generally, the Webster-Ashburton Treaty resolved differences that could have precipitated a third Anglo-American war had they gone unattended; dealing with them brought not only resolution of the issues but greatly improved the relationship between the United States and Great Britain.

In other significant foreign relations matters, Tyler persuaded Denmark to reduce its heavy tariff on world commerce, and in 1843 he protected the independence of the Sandwich Islands (Hawaii) against the British and French colonial interests by invoking the Monroe Doctrine. The protection of the Sandwich Islands brought them into the American sphere of influence, where they have remained since. A great part of the reason that the Sandwich Islands were of value to the United States was the country's growing interest in trade with China. Indeed, one of the Tyler administration's great accomplishments in foreign relations was the negotiation of the conspicuously favorable Treaty of Wanghia, ratified in 1844. This first treaty between the United States and China gave the United States most favored nation trading status, access to five important trading ports, fixed tariffs, and extraterritorial rights for its citizens living in some parts of China. In addition to the benefits of trade, China had hoped to gain diplomatic support from the United States in resolving some of its own foreign relation problems, but this largely failed to materialize.

International endeavors and accomplishments aside, Tyler's administration was vilified by his political opponents at home. His presidency appeared bleak and lifeless until the "Rose of Long Island" walked into his life.

A Rose for Texas

Julia Gardiner, the daughter of New York Senator David Gardiner of Gardiner's Island, was called the "Rose of Long Island." Senator Gardiner had taken his two young daughters Julia and Margaret to Washington so that they could be introduced to Washington society. On February 7, 1843, Julia was one of thirteen guests invited to the White House for a quiet social gathering with the president.

Tyler Finds a New Love

The Gardiner sisters were quite active and successful in their social pursuits. President Tyler teased Julia and Margaret about the number of parties they had attended and the beaus they had attracted. The fifty-two-year-old Tyler was especially smitten by the dark-haired, flirtatious Julia. She was thirty years younger than he, but this did not discourage him. For two weeks following their visit to the White House, Tyler found ways to communicate with Julia, usually by relaying messages to her through his son Robert.

Washington's Birthday Ball was held on February 22, 1843, at the White House. Being the daughter of a senator, Julia was invited. She wore a white tarlatan dress and a crimson Greek cap with a dangling tassel. The president was so captivated by Julia that he whisked her off the dance floor, taking her away from a naval officer. Wisely, the naval officer did not voice his dissatisfaction to his Commander-in-Chief.

Tyler and Julia danced through the rooms of the White House and, as they moved about, Tyler asked Julia to marry him. A stunned Julia shook her head, "No, no, no," causing the tassel to tickle the president's face. When the ball was over, Julia decided not to tell her father about the president's proposal. She would keep quiet, but the City of Washington had already figured out that the president had fallen in love with the beautiful Julia Gardiner.

Before the Gardiners returned to New York in March, Tyler once again proposed marriage to Julia. This time he made his proposal in front of Margaret, Julia's sister. Julia confessed her true feelings of affection for the president, accepted his proposal, and told her parents the news. Julia's parents encouraged her not to set a date for a few months in case her feelings were to change, and she reluctantly agreed. Throughout the summer of 1843, Tyler worked on his pet project — the annexation of Texas — and wrote love letters to Julia.

The Proposal to Annex Texas

Soon after Mexico secured its independence from Spain in 1821, American immigrants began settling in Texas under a variety of programs authorized by the Mexican government and that of the state of Coahuila and Texas. Being located on the northeastern frontier of Mexico, far from the center of state and national power, the ties with the United States that these immigrants inevitably brought with them intensified into dominant social, economic, and eventually political allegiances. Texas declared itself independent of Mexico on March 2, 1836, and a few weeks later, on April 21, Sam Houston's Texan Army defeated the Mexican Army at the battle of San Jacinto, thereupon securing Texas's independence — at least for the time being. The United States and many European nations recognized Texas's sovereignty, but Mexico broke off diplomatic relations with the United States because of the support the United States had shown for the cause of Texas independence.

Even though Texas was free for the moment, the new nation was nonetheless vulnerable. The conflict with Mexico had left it financially drained and there remained the threat that Mexican President Santa Anna might reinvade the republic and reclaim it as a part of Mexico. Texas President Sam Houston, and much of the Texas population, wanted to join the United States and first requested to join the Union in December, 1836. Congress, however, declined to act favorably on the overture. Although the United States had long wanted Texas to help satisfy the country's growing appetite for westward expansion, the issue of admitting Texas was laced with the divisive question of slavery and the threat of war with Mexico.

Shortly after Tyler had taken office in 1841, he had approached Daniel Webster about the matter of incorporating Texas into the Union. Webster had vehemently opposed the idea because the government of Mexico had made clear the fact that it would not tolerate such an act. Mexico considered the Treaty of Velasco, upon which Texas based its claim of independence, fraudulent and invalid. To Mexico, Texas was a province in rebellion and, if it were to be annexed by the United States, Mexico would retaliate. Because of Webster's response, Tyler had dropped the issue. But later, after Webster resigned his cabinet position on May 8, 1843, Tyler again began to show interest in the annexation of Texas.

Despite his strong Jeffersonian ideals, Tyler believed in Manifest Destiny — the inevitability of the westward expansion of the United States. He regarded America's future as being dependent upon its ability to freely trade on the open world market. Expanding westward to the Pacific would benefit the country by providing it with new resources and seaports on the Pacific coast. Texas would be the next step in this westward quest.

Tyler's new Secretary of State, Abel P. Upshur, shared the president's enthusiasm for westward expansion and favored bringing Texas into the Union. In December, 1843, Upshur took an informal poll in Congress regarding the issue, and he concluded that two-thirds of the members would vote in favor of admitting Texas. Upshur told Tyler of his findings, and Tyler began negotiating the matter with his counterpart in Texas, Sam Houston. Because of the threat of retaliation from Mexico if Texas were fully annexed, however, Houston proposed an agreement that would provide Texas only with military protection by the United States. Upshur and Tyler complied with Houston's requests, and work began on the treaty to conclude the negotiations.

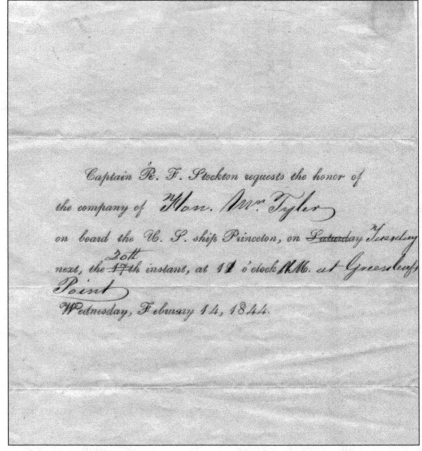

The invitation to President Tyler from Captain Stockton requesting the president to join him on board the Princeton *on February 20th, 1844, for a celebratory cruise on the Potomac River. The event actually took place on the 28th. (Courtesy Sherwood Forest Plantation)*

The Princeton *Disaster*

On February 28, 1844, some 350 invited guests joined Navy Captain Robert F. Stockton for a gala excursion down the Potomac River aboard the new steam frigate *Princeton*. President Tyler was among the guests, as were politicians, foreign diplomats, military officers, and others of the Washington elite — including Dolley Madison. Julia and Margaret Gardiner had returned to the capital from New York, and they too accompanied their father on the *Princeton* outing.

The high point of the excursion was to be the firing of the "Peacemaker," the world's largest naval gun, and everyone gathered on deck to witness the event. The Peacemaker was discharged for the cheering crowd twice, then the guests went below deck for food, drink, and merriment. As the ship passed Mount Vernon, George Washington's plantation, someone in the crowd suggested to Captain Stockton that the Peacemaker be fired one more time in honor of the first president. The captain agreed and went on deck followed by Senator Gardiner and some other guests. Julia remained below. Tyler started up the steps, but he stopped when his son-in-law, William Waller, began to sing.

The Peacemaker was fired once again. Within seconds, an officer shouted below for a surgeon. The Peacemaker had exploded! Smoke soon filtered below deck. Julia frantically tried to get up on deck to check on her father, but was stopped and told that her father was in heaven. Julia fainted.

Senator David Gardiner, Secretary of State Upshur, and Secretary of the Navy Thomas Gilmer were among the eight who died in the blast. Many others, including Captain Stockton, were injured. A rescue boat was quickly summoned to take the panic-stricken guests ashore.

President Tyler was carrying Julia across the gangway when she regained consciousness. Confused, Julia thrashed in the president's arms, nearly knocking both of them into the water. Fortunately, Tyler held his footing. Julia and Margaret were taken to the White House, while Tyler and Secretary of War William Wilkens remained on the *Princeton* to look after the deceased.

News of the tragedy spread quickly. Julia's mother, Julianna, and her two brothers, David Lyon and Alexander, glumly traveled to Washington. The bodies of the deceased lay at rest in the East Room of the White House, where over 20,000 people came to show their respects. A two-mile funeral procession was followed by services on Capitol Hill. Throughout this time of mourning, the president tenderly consoled the grief-stricken members of the Gardiner family.

Tyler Remarries

Julia was extremely saddened by her father's untimely death. Yet, it was during this time that she made the decision to marry John Tyler. Julianna consented to the wedding after expressing her financial concerns in a letter to the president. Politicians made very little money, and she wanted to make sure that, if her daughter married the president, she would be able to live in comfort similar to that which the Gardiner family had known for two centuries.

Seven weeks after the *Princeton* tragedy, June 26, 1844, was set as the date of the secret wedding. The small, private ceremony took place at the Episcopal Church of the Ascension in New York. Tyler invited Captain Stockton and a few other friends. His son John, Jr., was the only one of Tyler's children present. Julia's mother, sister, and two brothers also attended.

Julia wore a simple white dress. Atop her head, a gauze veil fell from a wreath of white flowers. She wore no jewelry as a sign of continued mourning for her father. The honeymoon consisted of a series of stops between New York and Tyler's newly acquired plantation, Sherwood Forest.

News of the wedding was published the next day, shocking everyone — including Tyler's daughters. Although his daughters and sons were aware of his intent to marry Julia, most did not know of the event until it was over.

John Tyler's marriage to Julia was a difficult adjustment for his daughters, who recently had lost their mother and who now had a stepmother close to their own ages. By contrast, Tyler's sons approved of their father's choice. Of course, many people wondered if he had married a woman who was too young. Even so, Julia quickly warmed the hearts of her skeptics. Her vivacious personality successfully charmed much of Washington.

Julia's mother scolded her for caressing Tyler in public and not tending to the unkempt White House. For three years, Congress had refused to appropriate funds to keep the White House updated and clean, and by 1844 it needed painting on the inside as well as the outside. Its pillars were stained with tobacco juice, and the rugs and draperies were worn and threadbare.

Using her own money, Julia refurbished and redecorated the White House, and then began to fulfill her role as First Lady or, as was the custom of the times, "Mrs. President Tyler." Julia enjoyed entertaining in the White House, and it was she who first asked that "Hail to the Chief" be played as a matter of official protocol when the president entered a room. Julia also established the custom of donating a portrait of the First Lady to the White House.

While Mrs. President Tyler was handling the decorating, John Tyler continued to pursue the idea of incorporating Texas into the Union. After Upshur's death, John C. Calhoun had become Secretary of State through a series of political maneuvers carried out during Tyler's honeymoon. Although he and Calhoun were friends, Tyler was disturbed by Calhoun's presence in his cabinet. He knew that Calhoun's pro-slavery views would complicate the Texas problem, so his appointment caused Tyler to rethink his strategy for the annexation. Tyler's position now became one of convincing Calhoun and others that the annexation of Texas was not about slavery, but rather was an issue bearing on coastal commerce and the future wealth and security of the United States.

The Election of 1844

Though elected as a Whig, Tyler had found himself — largely because of the machinations of Henry Clay — unwanted by that party soon after he became president, and so he returned to the Democratic party. Both he and James Knox Polk were candidates of the Democratic party for president in 1844, but because of the division in the Democratic party, Tyler believed that neither had a chance of being elected president. Instinctively, he knew that his presence as a Democratic candidate would split the party and thereby ensure the election of the Whig candidate, almost certainly to be Henry Clay. He therefore chose to use the campaign of 1844 as an element in his strategy to bring about the annexation of Texas.

Tyler set his plan into motion. He staged his own third-party political convention in the same city and at the same time as the Democratic convention. Using tactics similar to those that had been successful in the 1840 campaign, he provided large amounts of whiskey and displayed numerous banners which read "Tyler and Texas," and thereby was able to attract enough Democrats into his third party to force the Democratic party to take a position on the Texas issue.

Tyler's strategy had been successful. Though he would not be nominated himself, Tyler had forced the Democrats to publicly support bringing Texas into the Union. As Tyler had reasoned, the Democrats nominated Polk as their presidential candidate. As anticipated, he would be opposed by Henry Clay, the candidate of the Whig party, now seeking the presidency for the third time. Tyler withdrew his own third-party nomination and supported Polk, who — in a close race — won the election and became the country's eleventh president. Tyler had battled with Henry Clay for four long years, and in his own way, he finally had defeated him.

James K. Polk

The Annexation of Texas

Four years of personal attacks, political infighting, and personal tragedy while president had changed John Tyler. The gracious Virginia gentleman now was a very capable politician, able to out maneuver even the golden-tongued Henry Clay. During the final months of his presidency, Tyler would use all of his political skills to bring about congressional approval for the admission of Texas.

The Senate had turned down the annexation of Texas in 1842. Sam Houston realized that his young republic was still subject to reconquest by Mexico and, while the United States failed to act favorably to unite the two countries, he needed to protect Texas's security and interests. Toward this end, Houston took steps to strengthen relations between Texas and Great Britain. Houston hoped that Britain would influence the Mexican government to recognize and accept Texas independence, while Britain had interests in stifling the westward expansion of the United States and in having a stronger presence and greater influence on the continent itself.

Tyler responded to Houston's overtures to Britain by calling for a joint session of Congress. He declared that stronger diplomatic ties between Texas and Great Britain would be a risk to the national security of the United States, and he called for a joint resolution to admit Texas to statehood.

Julia Tyler joined in the fight. She spent many hours dining with and lobbying senators, representatives, and their wives — and encouraging them to support her husband on this matter. Julia's efforts as a hostess and John Tyler's political arm-twisting paid off when Congress passed the resolution to annex Texas on February 27, 1845. Tyler signed the measure on March 1, 1845, three days before he surrendered his office. To show Julia his appreciation, Tyler gave her

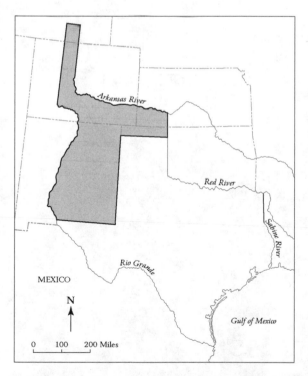

Texas at the time it was annexed by the United States in 1845. The shaded portion of Texas was transferred to the United States in 1850 in exchange for $10,000,000.00.

the historic golden pen which he used to sign the resolution that brought Texas into the Union. Julia made the pen into a necklace, and she wore it proudly — literally, to her grave, for she was buried with the necklace still in place around her neck.

Julia's greatest social engagement, however, was her husband's farewell ball on Wednesday, February 18, 1845. Two thousand people had been invited to the White House for this event, but 3000 arrived. A buffet supper and plenty of wine and champagne were served to the guests. Six hundred glowing candles illuminated the rooms of the White House as the scarlet-uniformed Marine band entertained the guests with music. Julia even persuaded her husband to dance the waltz, a dance which he once considered inappropriate. In a letter to her mother, Julia jokingly wrote, "They cannot say now that President Tyler is a president without a party. I have given him a party!"

The Abolitionist

The annexation of Texas had been the final and greatest moment of John Tyler's administration. In his moving farewell, he said:

> In 1840 I was called from my farm to undertake the administration of public affairs, and I foresaw that I was called to a bed of thorns. I now leave that bed which has afforded me little rest, and eagerly seek repose in the quiet enjoyments of rural life. . . . I rely on future history, and on the candid and impartial judgment of my fellow citizens, to award me the meed due to honest and conscientious purposes to serve my country. . . . The acquisition of Texas is a measure of the greatest importance. Our children's children will live to realize the vast benefits conferred on our country by the union of Texas with this Republic. . . .

Tyler had survived a "baptism by fire" as president, and he literally left in a blaze. As he and Julia departed from Washington for Sherwood Forest, a huge fire destroyed the National Theater and the surrounding buildings. It was an unfortunate, yet fittingly, symbolic end to Tyler's presidency.

Retirement at Sherwood Forest

Life at Sherwood Forest was pleasant, and Tyler enjoyed his retirement. He and Julia relished in the comforts of their plantation located on the banks of the James River. In 1845, Tyler designed and added a sixty-eight-foot-long ballroom so that he, Julia, and their guests could dance the Virginia Reel. With this expansion, the three-hundred-foot-long house became the longest frame dwelling in America.

Julia joyfully decorated Sherwood Forest. Throughout the first fifteen years following their departure from Washington, she wrote letters to family members in New York arranging for purchases of "wants" for their residence. She carefully landscaped the plantation and, during these years, seven children were born.

While Julia handled the domestics, Tyler lived the life of a gentleman planter. Wearing his oversized Panama hat, he supervised the production of wheat and corn on his plantation. In 1860, Tyler served as Chancellor of The College of William and Mary.

The James River was a lifeline for the Tylers — upon it moved mail, news, goods, trade, and travelers. Their small bright blue boat, the *Pocahontas*, had been a farewell gift to Tyler from his friend, Commodore Beverly Kennon. Tyler and Julia enjoyed the *Pocahontas* and often used it to visit their neighbors along the river. Much of the Tyler's leisure time at home was spent on the piazza where Julia enjoyed playing her guitar and singing while John practiced his fiddle. Life was peaceful at Sherwood Forest and good to the Tylers, but sadly the rest of the country was moving towards war.

The Gray Room, or parlor, of Sherwood Forest Plantation was used for family activities and informally to entertain guests. President Tyler's breakfast table is prominent in the center of the room. (Courtesy Sherwood Forest Plantation)

The birdbath that Julia Gardiner Tyler purchased for the south lawn at Sherwood Forest. (Photograph by Jane C. Walker)

The Slavery Issue Worsens

As Tyler had once predicted, the Missouri Compromise of 1820 had settled little. For the next thirty years, the slavery issue had persisted and tensions had grown on both sides. In 1850, as the division grew worse, the Great Triumvirate of Clay, Webster, and Calhoun was summoned to Capitol Hill. All three were old, feeble, and ill, and all would be dead within two years — but at this moment they still represented an extremely powerful and dedicated wealth of national political experience and commitment to their country.

The problem faced by the three men was to devise a way to mesh the slavery issue with the territory that the United States had gained through the Mexican War in 1845 and 1846. The plan which they developed was called the Compromise of 1850. In it, California would become a free state, New Mexico and Utah would have no slavery restrictions, there would be no slavery interference in the District of Columbia, and the Fugitive Slave Law — which stated that any runaway slave found in a Northern state was to be captured and returned to his master — would be enforced. Tyler admired the efforts of the authors of this compromise, but he believed that the problems associated with slavery would linger despite the remedies the three learned men had proposed.

This compromise was not supported by northern abolitionists; they considered slavery immoral, and not merely a problem to be managed by political processes. On June 5, 1851, an antislavery journal — the *National Era* — began publishing, in serial form, the novel *Uncle Tom's Cabin* that had been written by an unfamiliar author named Harriet Beecher Stowe. Within a year, over 300,000 copies of the book had been sold. It was then translated into thirty-six languages and was adapted as a play that drew large audiences. In later years, President Abraham Lincoln, upon meeting Mrs. Stowe, would say, "So this is the little woman who made the big war."

The abolitionist movement spread throughout the Union, encouraged from across the Atlantic where, especially in Great Britain, anti-slavery sentiment was strong. The Duchess of Sutherland and other ladies of Britain sent an open letter supporting abolition to American news and literary media in hopes that the sensitive Southern ladies might come to share their views and would then demand an end to slavery.

Julia had been born in the North but quickly adjusted to Southern ways. She fumed over the Duchess of Sutherland's letter. In the February, 1853, issue of the *Southern Literary Messenger*, she published a rebuttal to the ladies of England. In it, she said that the slave system at Sherwood Forest and other James River plantations bore little resemblance to that of Stowe's novel. Julia did not defend the morality of slavery, but she did point out that the slaves were better kept, fed, and clothed than the depressed white laborers of London.

Julia ended her article by attacking the British abolitionist interference in American affairs, and she reminded the English ladies that slavery was first brought to America by British colonial administrators. Julia's powerful article was applauded in both the South and the North, and letters of praise flooded Sherwood Forest. Some people thought that the furor created by Stowe's novel had been squashed, but John Tyler knew better.

On March 6, 1857, the Supreme Court issued its Dred Scott decision in which the court ruled that slaves were not citizens and, therefore, the Missouri Compromise was unconstitutional. Because of this ruling, any state could now choose to permit slavery, and slavery could now legally expand westward into the new territories.

Southerners were elated, but Tyler was not. He agreed with the court's decision that free Negroes were not citizens and that Congress had no right to restrict slavery. However, Tyler also realized that slavery in the western territories would be impractical from topographical and climatic standpoints, just as it had been in the North. He also believed that the Dred Scott ruling would add more fuel to the growing abolitionist movement.

Tyler's assessment was accurate. In October, 1859, an unstable John Brown and his handful of abolitionist followers seized the federal arsenal at Harpers Ferry, Virginia, in an attempt to secure land and establish a safe haven in the mountains of Virginia for free blacks and runaway slaves. In response, President James Buchanan sent a company of United States Marines to Harpers Ferry. The marines, led by Colonel Robert E. Lee, captured Brown and his men. After a speedy trial, Brown was convicted of murdering a marine and committing treason against the Commonwealth of Virginia, and he was hanged at Charles Town, Virginia, on December 2, 1859.

The extremist Brown was dead, but the abolition movement he had supported was not. Influential New England writers such as Ralph Waldo Emerson and Henry David Thoreau praised Brown as a martyr and a hero. While Northern bells tolled and services were held in honor of Brown, the Southern aristocracy panicked. In Charles City County, Virginia, where Sherwood Forest was located and where Negroes outnumbered whites two to one, Tyler and other plantation owners stocked their arms and organized a mounted patrol to protect their families and properties from a possible slave uprising. The slave rebellion that Brown had envisioned, however, never materialized.

The Sectionalist

The presidential election of 1860 was anything but docile. Sectional divisions were so great that the Democratic party was split. Northern Democrats nominated Stephen A. Douglas as their candidate. Remembering that Douglas had blocked the admission of Kansas as a slave state, however, the Southern Democrats nominated John C. Breckinridge of Kentucky as their candidate. This division within the Democratic party led to the election of Abraham Lincoln, the nominee of the new National Republican party.

The Deep South States Secede

Tyler had feared that if Lincoln won the presidential election, the Southern states would secede from the United States. Many Southerners, especially those in South Carolina, viewed the Republicans as an abolitionist party. On December 20, 1860, shortly after Lincoln's election, South Carolina voted to secede. Mississippi, Alabama, Georgia, Florida, Louisiana, and Texas joined South Carolina within the first two months of 1861. These seven states formed a new nation which they named the Confederate States of America, and they wrote their own constitution which permitted slavery and emphasized the sovereignty of individual states. Soon thereafter, they elected Jefferson Davis as their temporary president.

From his plantation home, Tyler watched as his prediction came true. Now, Virginia was in a frenzy as its leaders considered whether they, too, should secede. As a former president, Tyler supported the preservation of the Union, and he advised Virginians either to sell their slaves or move to the Deep South if they wished to continue owning them. Tyler, however, chose to stay in Virginia and to hope for a political compromise.

The Peace Conference

In a final attempt to prevent war before Lincoln took office, President Buchanan, acting upon a proposal of the Virginia Assembly, directed the federal government to hold a peace conference in Washington to consider compromises that might preserve the Union. President Buchanan asked former President John Tyler, who had originated the idea of the conference in the first place, to serve as his special commissioner to the gathering. About the same time, Tyler was asked to be the Virginia commissioner to the conference and a Charles City County delegate to the state convention which was considering the matter of secession.

James Buchanan

The aging Tyler was quite flattered to be chosen for these three positions. He believed that these would be his last opportunities to serve his country. Julia also was proud to have her husband return to politics, and she looked forward to returning to Washington with the realization that her husband was again needed.

Floods of letters, telegrams, and visits from concerned people greeted the Tylers upon their arrival in the capital. Julia enjoyed the excitement along with the numerous parties and balls which accompanied the conference. Her husband, though, had difficulty keeping up with the social obligations. The pressure of trying to save the Union and his recurring digestive problem were taking their toll upon the seventy-year-old former president.

Despite his wavering health, Tyler was unanimously elected president of the conference on February 5, 1861. All states were welcomed, but as Tyler had anticipated, the seven states that had seceded were not present, and their absence concerned him. As the free states at the conference outnumbered the slave states fourteen to seven, the prospects for devising a compromise and persuading the other states to return to the Union appeared bleak.

Tyler opened the conference with a speech, and for the first time in a formal public forum he acknowledged that he now believed the Constitution to be a growing document. He recognized the need for a new constitutional amendment that would meet the demands of a country that now had grown to include thirty million citizens, and he asked the delegates to work together to accomplish this goal. The delegates agreed and applauded Tyler.

On February 6, 1861, the delegates began their deliberations on a proposed constitutional amendment that would prevent a civil war. While they worked, an emotionally drained President Buchanan summoned Tyler to help him solve the Fort Sumter stalemate. Fort Sumter was a small Union fort on an island in Charleston Harbor, immediately east of Charleston, South Carolina. South Carolinians had felt both threatened and irritated by the presence of American soldiers in the fort and, considering themselves no longer a part of the Union, they demanded that these symbols of United States sovereignty be removed from their state.

Tyler urged Buchanan to reduce the force of eighty-odd men in the fort to six, but President Buchanan refused. Instead, Buchanan asked Tyler to contact the governor of South Carolina and assure him that the United States wanted only peace. Tyler agreed to do this, and a successful understanding was reached with the governor. A grateful Buchanan paid a personal call on Tyler to thank him.

Though the Fort Sumter crisis had been quietly resolved, the peace conference was anything but quiet. Sparks flew, tempers flared, and Tyler had difficulty controlling the rowdy delegates. While Northern extremists refused to permit any extension of slavery into the territories, Southern spokesmen argued that an extension of slavery would be the only possible way to bring the seven seceded states back into the Union. By February 13, 1861, Tyler had begun to believe that there was very little hope that a peaceful political compromise could be reached, and his thoughts turned to the possibility that Virginia might now consider seceding, a view that had been exacerbated during his only encounter with president-elect Lincoln. While speaking to the conference delegates, Lincoln had been asked a question about slavery, to which he responded, "In a choice of evils, war may not always be the worst." This statement infuriated Tyler.

Four days after the meeting with Lincoln, on February 27, the peace conference delegates reached a consensus and drafted a constitutional amendment, which in turn was sent to Congress. The amendment provided that slavery be prohibited north of the thirty-six degree, thirty minute parallel. This was similar to Clay's old Missouri Compromise of 1820, held to be unconstitutional by the Dred Scott case of 1857. As Tyler had expected, Congress did not approve the amendment. Frustrated and saddened, Tyler returned to his home in Virginia.

Virginia Joins the Confederacy

Abraham Lincoln was inaugurated as the nation's sixteenth president on March 4, 1861. The following day, Tyler's nineteen-year

old granddaughter, Letitia, hoisted a Confederate flag atop Alabama's capitol. Tyler wanted the flag to fly over the Virginia capitol, but Virginia was still a member state of the Union and had strong Union ties.

Even though Tyler usually disagreed with Lincoln, he recognized Lincoln's strategy on Fort Sumter as a masterstroke. Lincoln not only left the fort manned, but he sent additional troops and munitions and predicted that the South Carolinians would retaliate against the reinforced garrison —

Abraham Lincoln

and they did. On April 12, South Carolina fired on the Union fort with cannons. Fort Sumter returned fire, and after thirty-three hours of fighting, Fort Sumter surrendered. South Carolinians cheered the victory, but Tyler knew that Lincoln had won. He had rallied the North to his position; there would be war with the Confederate States!

On April 17, 1861, Virginia — in response to President Lincoln's mobilization of troops — seceded from the Union, and Tyler's family became very active supporters of the Confederacy. His sons from his first marriage were too old for combat, but Robert was appointed Register of the Treasury of the Confederacy. Major John Tyler, Jr., served as an assistant to the Secretary of War, and Tazewell Tyler became a surgeon in the Confederate States Army. Tyler's son-in-law took a post in the Confederate States Navy Department, while two of his grandsons, children of Tyler's deceased daughter Mary, joined the Army of Northern Virginia. One later received a citation for wounds suffered at Gettysburg. Two other grandsons, from Tyler's daughter Elizabeth, joined the Confederate Army; the younger one would die in combat. Julia enlisted her young sons David and Alexander in the Charles City County Junior Guard and, at the ages of thirteen and fourteen, then members of the Confederate infantry, they fought in the Battle of New Market. Both were also present when General Robert E. Lee surrendered his command at Appomattox in April, 1865.

Like so many families in America, the Gardiner family found itself divided by the Civil War. Even though they were from the North, both Julia and her mother were sympathetic to the Southern cause. Julia's nephew, however, served as a colonel in the New York Sixth Brigade, National Guard, and her only surviving brother David supported the Union cause.

Tyler's Death

Six months into the war, John Tyler had re-entered politics. In November, 1861, he was appointed to a seat in the Confederate House of Representatives. During the first week of January, 1862, Tyler left for Richmond to take his seat in the Confederate House of Representatives. Julia had planned to join her husband the following week. On the night of January 9, Julia dreamed that Tyler was dangerously ill, and he was in a bed that she had never seen before. Frightened by the dream, she left for Richmond the next morning with her youngest daughter, Pearl. She arrived at the Exchange Hotel that evening and found her husband pleasantly surprised and quite well.

Three days later, on January 12, Tyler awoke feeling dizzy and nauseated. He eventually fainted. A doctor who was in the hotel at this time treated the seventy-one-year-old former president. He believed that Tyler was suffering from bronchitis and a liver attack. In reality, he had experienced a stroke.

During the next five days, Tyler remained in the hotel. He received visits from a few friends and from his sons Robert and Tazewell. Much to his disappointment, Tyler decided that he would have to miss the opening sessions of the Confederate Congress.

Tyler had decided to go home to Sherwood Forest to recuperate, but on the night of January 17, 1862, before he had left Richmond, he began to gasp for air. Awakened by the sounds of her husband, Julia again summoned the doctor. When the doctor appeared, Tyler told him that he was dying. Julia then tilted a glass of brandy toward her husband's lips. He looked up, smiled, and died at 12:15 AM in the bed that Julia had seen in her dream.

Two days later, in a black-draped hall of the Confederate Congress, Tyler's body lay in state. Thousands of mourners filed past the open casket, which had been draped with a Confederate flag. An evergreen and white rose wreath was placed on his chest.

On the following day, Tyler's funeral service was held at Saint Paul's Episcopal Church in Richmond. After the service, a three-mile-long cortege made up of 150 carriages solemnly followed the hearse through the gloomy, drizzling rain to Richmond's Hollywood Cemetery. John Tyler was then laid to rest beside another Virginia president, James Monroe, in the cemetery overlooking the James River.

Considering him a rebel, official Washington gave no notice of the former president's death. Though John Tyler, a Virginia gentleman and the tenth president of the United States, died peacefully, the Civil War roared on — destroying his beloved Virginia and mercilessly killing young Americans on both sides.

Epilogue

Death saved John Tyler from the horrors of war. Julia — widowed at forty-one years of age and the mother of seven young children — was not so fortunate. She was faced with mounting debts, the demands of managing a large plantation with fluctuating numbers of seventy to ninety hands, and a war in her own back yard. She was understandably frightened, but for the next twenty-seven years she put aside her fears and bravely fought back through illnesses, family tragedies, and court battles. She never remarried.

Julia remained at Sherwood Forest through the first part of the war. Beginning in 1863, she tried to sell Sherwood Forest in order to pay the taxes imposed by the Union forces, but she was never able to do so. She did, however, succeed in raising the necessary money to pay the elevated taxes.

During the early years of the war, Julia took at least two trips to New York to visit her mother. On one trip, in November, 1863, she traveled on *The Cornucopia*, a ship that ran the Union naval blockade and traveled to Bermuda, then to New York. On this trip she successfully smuggled five bales of cotton through the Union lines to Bermuda where they were sold. That same year, Julia and five of her children temporarily moved to Staten Island, New York, in an effort to escape the war. When Union troops moved through Charles City County in the spring of 1864, violating orders to respect the property of former presidents, they stripped the land, destroyed some furnishings, and vandalized the mansion at Sherwood Forest. Sailors aboard a vessel on the James River rescued the house before extensive damage occurred, so the building itself remained largely intact and, by the summer of 1864, was temporarily converted by federal authorities into a school for white and Negro children. By this time, Tyler's former slaves had moved away.

Julia continued to live on Staten Island until 1871, when she moved to Georgetown in the District of Columbia. She had wanted both to return to the Washington social life and to be closer to Sherwood

The gravesite of John Tyler in Hollywood Cemetery, Richmond, Virginia, and the memorial shaft erected in 1915. (Photograph by Jane C. Walker)

Forest. While in Washington, Julia petitioned for a federal pension as a president's widow; although she was unsuccessful, Congress did award annual pensions of $5000 to the widows of former United States presidents beginning in 1882, following the assassination of President James Garfield.

On July 10, 1889, Julia died of a stroke at the Exchange Hotel in Richmond, Virginia — the same hotel in which President Tyler had died. She is buried beside her husband at Hollywood Cemetery. According to her wishes, Julia lies at rest wearing the "immortal golden Texas pen" around her neck, a final tribute to her pride in the political accomplishments of her husband, President John Tyler.

For many years, there was no official monument at the grave of John Tyler. Finally, in 1915, Congress honored the tenth president by erecting an imposing twenty-foot-tall marble shaft with President John Tyler's bust mounted on the front. His birthday, March 29, is commemorated in a public ceremony conducted at Hollywood Cemetery by the United States government.

Sherwood Forest plantation remains within the Tyler family. John Tyler's grandson, Harrison Ruffin Tyler, and his wife restored the estate in the mid-1970s to its original elegance. The plantation is located on Virginia State Highway 5 — the John Tyler Memorial Highway — in Charles City County. The formal rooms of the mansion and the surrounding fifty acres of land are open to the public as a museum commemorating the life and times of President John Tyler. Sherwood Forest Plantation is a National Historic Landmark, is listed on the National Register of Historic Places, and is a Virginia Historic Landmark.

Important Dates
in the Life of John Tyler

March 29, 1790   Born at Greenway Plantation in Charles City County, Virginia

July 1807   Graduated from The College of William and Mary

1809   Practiced law as an attorney

1811–1816   Served as member of the Virginia House of Delegates

March 29,1813   Married Letitia Christian

1816–1821   Served as member of the United States House of Representatives

1823–1825   Served as member of the Virginia House of Delegates

1825–1826   Served as Governor of Virginia

1827–1836   Served as United States Senator

1835   Elected President *pro tempore* of the United States Senate

November 4, 1840   Elected Vice President of the United States

March 4–

April 4, 1841   Served as vice president to William Henry Harrison

1841–1845   Served as tenth President of the United States

1841   Tyler's (Harrison's) original cabinet resigned, except for Daniel Webster

1842   Webster-Ashburton Treaty with Great Britain concluded; Letitia Christian Tyler died

1843	Recognized and protected independence of the Sandwich Islands (Hawaii)
June 26, 1844	Married Julia Gardiner
1844	Treaty of Wanghia signed with China
February 27, 1845	Congress voted to annex Texas; annexation signed into law by Tyler on March 1
March 3, 1845	Florida admitted as twenty-seventh state
March 4, 1845	Ended term as President of the United States
1850s	Practiced law from his home, managed Sherwood Forest Plantation, held public offices
1860	Served as Chancellor of The College of William and Mary
April 12, 1860	Delivered eulogy to Henry Clay at unveiling of Clay's statue in Richmond
1861	Served as president of the peace conference
1861–1862	Served as member of the Confederate States Congress
January 18, 1862	Died in Richmond, Virginia

Tyler Trivia

1) John Tyler was a president of many firsts, including:
   - The first president born after the Revolutionary War.
   - The first and only time in history that a president of the United States and his vice president were born in the same state and county: President William Henry Harrison and Vice President John Tyler both were born in Charles City County, Virginia.
   - The first and only time in history that a president of the United States and his vice president have been closely related: President William Henry Harrison and Vice President John Tyler were cousins by marriage.
   - The first vice president to succeed to the presidency upon the death of a president.
   - The first president who served without a vice president.
   - The first president to be widowed while in office.
   - The first president to re-marry while in office.
   - The first president to use the telegraph.
   - The first president to establish formal diplomatic relations with China.
   - The first president to have "Hail to the Chief" played as official protocol when he entered a room.
   - The first president to have his wife, first lady Julia Gardiner Tyler, donate a portrait of herself to the White House.
   - The first and only president to live in a state that seceded from the country he had served.

2) John Tyler was the president with the most children, fifteen:
   - Eight by Letitia: Mary (b. 1815), Robert (b. 1816), John (b.

1819), Letitia (b. 1821), Elizabeth (b. 1823), Anne (b. 1825), Alice (b. 1827), Tazewell (b. 1830)

- Seven by Julia: David Gardiner (b. 1846), John Alexander (b. 1848), Julia (b. 1849), Lachlan (b. 1851), Lyon Gardiner (b. 1853), Robert Fitzwalter (b. 1856), Pearl (b. 1860)

3) Both John and Julia Tyler died in the Exchange Hotel, Richmond, Virginia.

4) John Tyler is buried near United States President James Monroe and President of the Confederate States Jefferson Davis in Hollywood Cemetery in Richmond, Virginia.

5) Sherwood Forest is the longest frame dwelling in America; it is 300 feet long.

6) Sherwood Forest is the only president's house continuously owned by direct descendants of the president.

7) Places named after John Tyler include:
- John Tyler Memorial Highway, Virginia.
- John Tyler Community College, Virginia.
- Tyler County, West Virginia.
- Tyler, Texas.
- Tyler Junior College, Tyler, Texas.

Bibliography

Bowers, Claude G. *John Tyler; Address by Hon. Claude G. Bowers of New York at the Unveiling of the Bust of President Tyler in the State Capitol, Richmond, Virginia, June 16, 1931.* Richmond, VA: Richmond Steam Press, 1932.

Chitwood, Oliver Perry. *John Tyler: Champion of the Old South.* Newton, CT: Political Biography Press, 1939.

Fraser, Hugh Russell. *Democracy in the Making: The Jackson-Tyler Era.* Indianapolis, IN: Bobbs-Merrill, ca. 1938.

Gantz, Richard A. *Henry Clay and the Harvest of Bitter Fruit: The Struggle with John Tyler, 1841–1842.* Ph.D. Dissertation, Indiana University, 1986.

Lambert, Oscar Doane. *Presidential Politics in the United States, 1841–1844.* Durham, NC: Duke University Press, 1936.

Remini, Robert V. *Henry Clay: Statesman of the Union.* New York, NY: W. W. Norton and Co., 1991.

Seager, Robert I. *And Tyler Too: A Biography of John and Julia Gardiner Tyler.* New York, NY: McGraw-Hill, 1963.

Tyler, Harrison Ruffin. "The Tyler, Texas Sesquicentennial." Speech Delivered to the Tyler, Texas, Sesquicentennial. April 19, 1995 [Typescript on file at Sherwood Forest Plantation].

Tyler, Lyon G. *The Letters and Times of the Tylers.* Richmond, VA: Whittet & Shepperson, 1884-1896.

Index